LEARNING FROM BIBLE GRANDPARENTS

BRIAN JOHNSTON

Copyright © Hayes Press 2017

All rights reserved. No part of this book may be reproduced, stored in a retrieval system, or transmitted in any form, without the written permission of Hayes Press.

Published for Search For Truth by:

HAYES PRESS Publisher, Resources & Media,

The Barn, Flaxlands

Royal Wootton Bassett

Swindon, SN4 8DY

United Kingdom

www.hayespress.org

Unless otherwise indicated, all Scripture quotations are from the New American Standard Bible®, (NASB®) Copyright © 1960, 1962, 1963, 1968, 1971, 1972, 1973, 1975, 1977, 1995 by The Lockman Foundation. Used by permission. (www.Lockman.org). All rights reserved. Scriptures marked NIV are from the New International Version®, NIV® Copyright © 1973, 1978, 1984, 2011 by Biblica, Inc.™ Used by permission. All rights reserved worldwide.

ISBN 978-1911433491

10 9 8 7 6 5 4 3 2 1

CHAPTER ONE: THE GRANDFATHER WHO COULDN'T LET GO OF HIS BITTERNESS

Someone has said that bitterness or bitter resentment is like a beach-ball that we try to submerge in water; no matter what we try, it bobs back up. It all starts out when an offence gets 'under our skin' - probably because we've interpreted the offence as intentional. Like a goal scored in a televised football game, we replay it in our minds. What happens is that each time we replay it, it gets etched more vividly in our memory. Brooding on it means it's likely we'll share it freely with any sympathetic audience. Of course, when we do that we stoke up the fire of resentment. It doesn't take long before we find ourselves cringing whenever we hear the offending person's name mentioned. We find ourselves looking for additional reasons, real or imagined, to dislike the offender. And so we end up forming successive layers of bitterness over the original irritation – something like the way an oyster does. The difference is that the end result is not a thing of beauty.

In his book, *Lee: The Last Years*, Charles Flood reports that after the Civil War, Robert E. Lee visited a Kentucky lady who took him to the remains of a grand old tree in front of her house. There she bitterly lamented the fact that its limbs and trunk had been destroyed by Federal artillery fire. She looked to Lee for a word condemning the North or at least sympathizing with her loss. After a brief silence, Lee said, 'Cut it down, my dear Madam, and forget it.' It's better to let go of the injustices of the past than to allow them to remain, let bitterness take root, and so poison the rest of our life.

Perhaps one man who would have benefited from such deep insight is Ahithophel, who we encounter in the life story of king David, his name forever intertwined with the most shameful episode in David's life. At this point, I should sound a caution that the following reconstruction depends on assuming that the same name repeated in Scripture is referring to the same person. Of course, it's quite possible that there were contemporaries of the same name.

The Ahithophel I have in mind is David's counselor, who betrayed him and joined the conspiracy of Absalom. Absalom was the son of David who rebelled against his father and tried to take his throne. Ahithophel's wisdom was proverbial (2 Samuel 16:23), and it seems clear that he didn't take a backseat in the rebellion against David (2 Samuel 15:12). What could have given him the motivation for this treachery? We know Absalom's – and I'll leave you to re-familiarize yourself with that from this part of the Bible – but what motivated Ahithophel? Some suggest (and this is where the caution about his assumed identity fits in) that we need look no further than to identify him as the same Ahithophel who was the grandfather of Bathsheba; for she was the daughter of Eliam (2 Samuel 11:3), and an Eliam, the son of Ahithophel the Gilonite, is listed as one of David's valiant men (2 Samuel 23:34).

This is why we began this chapter with some introductory discussion of bitterness. This plausible reconstruction suggests that Ahithophel retained a certain bitterness toward David, the murderer of his grandson by marriage – king David being the corrupter of his granddaughter. (Others note, however, that the timing seems tight for Ahithophel to have a married granddaughter at the time of David's great sin, and so we have to recognize that it's at least as possible to believe that there was more than one man in Israel named Eliam. It is certainly possible his main motivation might have been ambition for personal power.)

LEARNING FROM BIBLE GRANDPARENTS 3

If the Ahithophel who sided with Absalom against David is the same one who had a grand-daughter with whom David committed adultery, it may be worth reminding ourselves of David's darkest days. David's downward spiral deeper into sin began like this: "In the spring, at the time when kings go off to war, David sent Joab out with the king's men and the whole Israelite army. They destroyed the Ammonites and besieged Rabbah. But David remained in Jerusalem" (2 Samuel 11:1 NIV).

That's the innocent-looking start of the downward spiral that would affect the course of the rest of David's life. There's just the hint that David shouldn't have been there at that time. David was indulging himself at home when "... one evening he got up from his bed and walked around on the roof of the palace. From the roof he saw a woman bathing. The woman was very beautiful" (2 Samuel 11:2 NIV). There was nothing wrong with David walking round on the roof of his palace, as far as we know. A beautiful woman catches his eye - it's nothing more than an unintentional first glance. Still no problem – the problem was what David did with this thought. He "... sent someone to find out about her. The man said, "Isn't this Bathsheba, the daughter of Eliam and the wife of Uriah the Hittite?" (2 Samuel 11:3 NIV). At this point, now that he's found out the woman was married to one of his soldiers, David should have dropped all further romantic thoughts about the woman. But, unfortunately, he'd already allowed the temptation to gain too much strength to be easily resisted. Finally "... David sent messengers to get her. She came to him, and he slept with her ... Then she went back home. The woman conceived and sent word to David, saying, 'I am pregnant'" (2 Samuel 11:4,5 NIV).

David's sin was to get a lot worse before he confessed it. He first tried to fix it. He recalled Bathsheba's husband from battle and plied him with alcohol and tried to get the man to sleep with his wife. It didn't work, so he sent him back to battle with a sealed command in his hand: David's general was to contrive to get the enemy to kill this soldier, Bathsheba's husband. The man was sent on what was, in effect, a 'suicide mission'. He was killed in battle. David then took Bathsheba, now a widow, to be another of his wives. Problem solved? No, we read that all this was deeply displeasing to God. Although God forgave David when he repented, the incident wasn't forgotten, and David had to reap what he'd sown. His family life was troubled after this. David had lost the moral authority to deal with incest in his own family circle, and that would lead to Absalom, one of his sons, taking matters into his own hands, and eventually trying to take over the reins of power from David his father. It would be natural for Bathsheba's grandfather to seize this opportunity to pay David back. Perhaps he felt David had seemed to get away with it. Ahithophel had been an advisor to David, and his advice always seemed to be inspired. Now he turned to advise Absalom against his father, David:

> "Ahithophel said to Absalom, "I would choose twelve thousand men and set out tonight in pursuit of David. I would attack him while he is weary and weak. I would strike him with terror, and then all the people with him will flee. I would strike down only the king and bring all the people back to you. The death of the man you seek will mean the return of all; all the people will be unharmed" (2 Samuel 17:1-3).

The strategy he proposed was a call for bold action, and probably was the best strategy. Absalom, however, listened to other advice:

> "... Absalom said, "Summon also Hushai the Arkite, so we can hear what he has to say as well." When Hushai came to him, Absalom said, "Ahithophel has given this

advice. Should we do what he says? If not, give us your opinion." Hushai replied to Absalom, "The advice Ahithophel has given is not good this time. You know your father and his men; they are fighters, and as fierce as a wild bear robbed of her cubs. Besides, your father is an experienced fighter; he will not spend the night with the troops. Even now, he is hidden in a cave or some other place. If he should attack your troops first, whoever hears about it will say, 'There has been a slaughter among the troops who follow Absalom.' Then even the bravest soldier, whose heart is like the heart of a lion, will melt with fear, for all Israel knows that your father is a fighter and that those with him are brave.

"So I advise you: Let all Israel, from Dan to Beersheba - as numerous as the sand on the seashore - be gathered to you, with you yourself leading them into battle. Then we will attack him wherever he may be found, and we will fall on him as dew settles on the ground. Neither he nor any of his men will be left alive. If he withdraws into a city, then all Israel will bring ropes to that city, and we will drag it down to the valley until not so much as a pebble is left." Absalom and all the men of Israel said, 'The advice of Hushai the Arkite is better than that of Ahithophel.' For the Lord had determined to frustrate the good advice of Ahithophel in order to bring disaster on Absalom" (2 Samuel 17: 5-14).

Ahithophel was not used to having his advice rejected, and also perhaps realized that the cause of Absalom was lost by not following it; and so he went to his home and hanged himself (2 Samuel 17:23). A tragic death, quite possibly due to the fact that here was someone who never got over his bitterness. This shows how we can't afford to hold onto bitterness and resentment against others, because it becomes the root of other problems. The Bible says in effect, 'Watch out for such bitterness!' (Hebrews 12:15). In fact, we're told to 'look diligently' for it, and that implied level of scrutiny is consistent with the fact that our bitterness may not be so obvious to us, and being unaware of it makes us all the more susceptible to its danger.

As we've illustrated in our reconstruction of the sad case of Bathsheba's grandfather, bitterness, if improperly handled, causes trouble - and that can take the form of physical, mental or spiritual problems. For example, in his book, *None of These Diseases*, S. I. McMillen claims that 'Anger, unhandled, will show itself in at least 50 diseases.' He also writes: 'The moment I start hating a person I become that person's slave. I can't enjoy life ... he controls my thoughts ... I can't escape his/her grasp on my mind. He or she may be many miles away, [but] always in my mind.' This leads onto how bitterness can also show up in our mental condition. It's really displaced anger. We can be angry at other things, other people and other objects, without realizing it all stems from some bitterness we're nursing. We experience no joy, no creativity, no positivity flowing through our lives - all because there's resentment there.

We're also affected spiritually when bitterness is not resolved. How? It can be by an inability to accept God's love or a doubting of our relationship to God. Ray Burke has written a book called *Anger - Diffusing the Bomb*, and in it he says that each time he dealt with those who doubted God's love for them, somewhere along the line he discovered they harboured bitterness against God, or someone. When this was dealt with and resolved, their ability to accept God's love and forgiveness returned. What better words can we conclude with, other than ... "Let all bitterness and wrath and anger and clamor and slander be put away from you, along with all malice. Be kind to one another, tender-hearted, forgiving each other, just as God in Christ also has forgiven you" (Ephesians 4:31-32).

CHAPTER TWO: A GRANDSON WHO WOULD SEE THE REVERSAL OF HIS GRANDFATHER'S SADNESS

"Now the Israelites went out to fight against the Philistines. The Israelites camped at Ebenezer, and the Philistines at Aphek. The Philistines deployed their forces to meet Israel, and as the battle spread, Israel was defeated by the Philistines, who killed about four thousand of them on the battlefield. When the soldiers returned to camp, the elders of Israel asked, 'Why did the Lord bring defeat on us today before the Philistines? Let us bring the ark of the Lord's covenant from Shiloh, so that he may go with us and save us from the hand of our enemies.' So the people sent men to Shiloh, and they brought back the ark of the covenant of the Lord Almighty, who is enthroned between the cherubim. And Eli's two sons, Hophni and Phinehas, were there with the ark of the covenant of God. When the ark of the Lord's covenant came into the camp, all Israel raised such a great shout that the ground shook. Hearing the uproar, the Philistines asked, 'What's all this shouting in the Hebrew camp?'

When they learned that the ark of the Lord had come into the camp, the Philistines were afraid. "A god has come into the camp," they said. "Oh no! Nothing like this has happened before. We're doomed! Who will deliver us from the hand of these mighty gods? They are the gods who struck the Egyptians with all kinds of plagues in the wilderness. Be strong, Philistines! Be men, or you will be subject to the Hebrews, as they have been to you. Be men, and fight!" So the Philistines fought, and the Israelites were defeated and every man fled to his tent. The slaughter was very great; Israel lost thirty thousand foot soldiers. The ark of God was captured, and Eli's two sons, Hophni and Phinehas, died" (1 Samuel 4:1-11 NIV).

The youthful figure watching the procession must surely have been nervous. He'd been raised in a God-fearing family. So much so, that his entire life – which was now stretching ahead of him – was given over to serving the LORD. Why was he nervous? And what was this procession? It was the Israelite army setting out to engage with their arch-rivals, the deadly enemy they knew as the Philistines. But why was the youth nervous? Was there any danger he would be conscripted? No, but something else had been; something he'd developed a deep sense of responsibility for. An unheard of thing was happening before his very eyes. The 'ark' belonging to God's covenant with his people was being taken by the soldiers into the theatre of war. The youth's heart sank, for he felt sure this wasn't at all the correct thing to do with the most sacred object, that was housed at Shiloh in those days. He had a deep sense of unease – and with good reason. But the elders of the people had been insistent that the presence of this sacred object, which symbolized the presence of God, was the very thing to make the difference and reverse recent defeats at the hands of their enemies.

One very good reason why young Samuel was nervous about this ill-conceived project was the obvious fact that the elders had never come to the priests to ask God's counsel. In the past, when there'd been a reversal of the nation's fortunes in any time of war, the leaders had inquired from God why he'd permitted such a defeat – after all he'd previously been the one to demonstrate his overwhelming power in the land of Egypt and at the extraordinary crossing of the Red Sea, which had seen their pursuers all drowned. In the past, this process of consultation had pinpointed failures which when corrected had restored victory. None of that this time. The elders had taken matters into their own hands, relying on their own idea of what was needed.

The problem was they were out of touch with God. Nearly all were in those closing days of the period when judges ruled the land of Israel. His people were chronically unresponsive, so God had been quiet for some time. But things were stirring afresh in the life of this young man, Samuel. Born in unusual circumstances into a priestly family, he would rise to become a judge himself, in fact the very last in a long line of judges. He'd be the one to anoint the very first king as the desired form of government changed. God had lately opened a line of communication with Samuel, and was moving powerfully in the young man's life. He was to become a force for revival in the nation. But not today - the people were in spiritual decline, almost free-fall, you might say.

Brought up in the environs of the nation's shrine at Shiloh, Samuel had been coached by his guardian, the old priest Eli. Eli had let things slip, and the way he managed his family affairs was not honouring to God. He indulged his sons' wrong-doing. He might not have been a bad man at heart, but he certainly wasn't a Moses who, when he saw family members dishonouring God, shattered the stone tables on which the law had been written by God, smashing them to the ground in his fury at human corruption. Eli was not of such stern stuff - he was a compromiser.

God himself would do what Eli had failed to do. In that procession we were talking about, - the one that took away the sacred ark into territory it was never intended for - Eli said goodbye to his two sons. He'd never see them again, for they would be killed in battle and the disastrous military campaign would be capped by the enemy capturing the ark of God. The news broke Eli's heart, and immediately afterwards his neck, as he fell backwards from his seat. Many years would pass before the ark would be restored to its proper place in the nation. Samuel never lived to see it back where it should have been. Nor did his sons, although they may well not have cared about that. You see, they were not like their father. Even with the poignant memory of Eli's carelessness with regard to his wicked sons, things didn't work out much better with Samuel's sons (see 1 Samuel 8:1-3).

Samuel had appointed them as judges, including Joel, his eldest, but they were dishonest men who perverted justice for the sake of bribes. How could history have repeated itself? Samuel's busy professional life wouldn't have helped, but the situation was so well-known that even the people could cite their failure as a justification for having a king to succeed Samuel – and not his sons. But brighter days lay ahead. A grandson was born to Samuel who would have thrilled his heart if he'd lived to see how he developed. This is what we read in 1 Chronicles 6:

> "Now these are those whom David appointed over the service of song in the house of the LORD, after the ark rested there. They ministered with song before the tabernacle of the tent of meeting, until Solomon had built the house of the LORD in Jerusalem; and they served in their office according to their order. These are those who served with their sons: From the sons of the Kohathites were Heman the singer, the son of Joel, the son of Samuel" (1 Chronicles 6:31-33).

I hope you picked out of there the words 'Heman the singer.' He was, we're told, a Kohathite Levite, a chief musician of the temple; and this is the main point, that he was a grandson of

Samuel. In fact, the inscription of the 88th Psalm bears his name. It seems he was given a leading part in the administration of the sacred services, certainly those aspects which involved music, judging by how the section was introduced. Heman is named among those in charge of the music (or 'the service of song'). This was after the ark had finally come to rest at Jerusalem. Saul, the first king, had never cared much if the ark was around or not (1 Chronicles 13:3), even after it had returned from enemy hands. So, it had lain for a long time in some backwater, we might say, in the field of the wood (Psalm 132:6). But David had a totally different approach. He knew it symbolised God's presence, and he didn't want to reign without it beside him at Jerusalem. So, he arranged to bring it up from where it had lain and bring it to Jerusalem, where it would remain ready for the temple his son Solomon would later build.

You may recall David's first misguided attempt to fetch the ark to Jerusalem. It was misguided due to him not following the instructions God had given to Moses, which specified in detail how the ark was to be transported. When they made a second attempt, this time 'going by the book' (1 Chronicles 16), all went well, to David's great delight. It was also at this time that David introduced music into the sacred service of God in association with the temple. I say David introduced it, but it was explicitly authorised by God. There can be no novelties in divine service, as Aaron's sons had tragically discovered. Heman, the grandson of Samuel, became one of the music leaders. He celebrated joyfully the full return of the ark his grandfather had seen departing.

Let's just take a moment to clarify what we've said there in case it's new to anyone. We've noted that musical instruments were first introduced into the service of God's house at the time of King David after about 500 hundred years of non-use. It wasn't that people had never dreamed of doing it before. Nationally, Israel had a tradition of using musical instruments to praise God in the commemoration of significant events like the Red Sea crossing when Miriam took the timbrel in her hand (Exodus 15:20). So, for hundreds of years instruments were readily available, and using them in civic celebration was something that was spontaneously natural to them, but throughout all that time neither instruments nor singing itself was a feature of the people's collective worship of God in Tabernacle service.

David was a skilled musician, and music seems surely to have enriched his personal life with God. This much comes through in his psalms. Yet for all his aptitude and eagerness to use musical instruments on occasions - for example as he attempted to bring the ark back to Jerusalem (2 Samuel 6:5) - the official incorporation of music (singing and instruments) had to await a very clear commandment from the Lord (2 Chronicles 29:25) - it wasn't David's initiative just because it suited him and since he happened to be gifted. So, the use of musical instruments was endorsed by God in later Old Testament times for Temple worship (2 Chronicles 29:27), but it's clear that the collective service of God's people as centred on the Temple was even then still restricted to far fewer instruments (1 Chronicles 15:16; 16:5,6; 2 Chronicles 29:25) than were permitted for more general, informal use by individuals or in social gatherings where God's Name was magnified (e.g. Psalm 149,150). In other words, there were instruments that weren't specified for Temple worship but which could find an acceptable, more informal, use in civic celebrations.

When we turn to the New Testament, the relevant commands (such as Ephesians 5:19; Colossians 3:16) and their exact wording emphasize singing (as opposed to accompanied singing):

> "... but be filled with the Spirit, speaking to one another in psalms and hymns and spiritual songs, singing and making melody with your heart to the Lord" (Ephesians 5:19).

> "Let the word of Christ richly dwell within you, with all wisdom teaching and admonishing one another with psalms and hymns and spiritual songs, singing with thankfulness in your hearts to God" (Colossians 3:16).

Historically, the very early Christian practice was, by all accounts, simply one of singing. But are we to take this 'singing only' formula as part of the New Testament pattern for church worship? The non-mention of the use of musical instruments throughout the first century New Testament churches of God in between two periods of their recorded use can be taken as highly significant.

Since instruments were available and had been (as we've seen) at times relevant, yet weren't evidently used in New Testament times, the argument from silence becomes a forceful one, showing that musical instruments are not part of the pattern for today. We might ask: 'Why not?' In this age, as distinct from when there was a physical house of God in which physical things assisted in the service, worship now is specifically spiritual (John 4:23,24). The Lord, in John chapter 4, talks about the character of worship in this age of spiritual sacrifices in a spiritual house (1 Peter 2:4,5) when he made the very positive statement that our worship should now be in spirit and truth. This would seem to imply the bypassing of additional things aimed at making the performance of the service more physically impressive. May we emulate Heman in his devotion to worship as biblically prescribed by God.

CHAPTER THREE: THE GRANDFATHER WHO WOULD HAVE BEEN SO DISAPPOINTED

The young man walked the winding path up the hill. He was heading into the hill country, known then as the hill country of Ephraim. This was a new venture for him, belonging as he did down in the town of Bethlehem, the city of David. But as he walked away he felt an exhilarating surge of freedom. The responsibilities of the service he'd been reared to perform with all its biblical rituals now lay behind him. He'd no particular destination in mind as he walked along. He was ready to explore whatever might come along. There was a real sense of excitement in not being able to predict what lay in store. The mood of these days was one of 'doing your own thing.' And that's what he fully intended to do. It'd be good to break with tradition, to find himself.

As it turned out, he didn't have to search long for an opportunity. An interesting challenge that seemed ideally suited to him presented itself quite early on. In one place where he found lodgings, his host enquired after his background, likely his accent gave him away as not being local. He began explaining that he was a Levite, belonging to that tribe of Israel which had by God's initiative been given the task, even the privilege, of assisting the priests in their duties around God's house. That should've been enough for any man, but somehow he'd grown weary of it. What was it that had bred discontent in the young man? The restless spirit of youth? A sense of needing to move with the times perhaps – did the careful instructions and provisions of the Law of Moses seem a bit outdated to him, I wonder? Had he inherited an adventurous spirit from his parents? It seems his father had married outside the tribe of Levi - married a woman of Judah, in fact, and so they weren't living in any one of the Levitical cities. Did this young man want to distance himself one stage further from living strictly as a Levite? Or was he simply making the same mistake each rising generation tends to make: by thinking there's greater freedom in exercising a choice that strays from God's prescribed path.

Once this young man had explained about his Levitical background, an idea suddenly flashed into the mind of his host. He, too, had kicked against God's laws, the ten commandments. For one thing, he'd broken the command against stealing. At one point he'd even stolen a large sum of money in silver from his own mother, but then his conscience had finally got the better of him and he'd returned it. With foolish indulgence, his mother had allowed him to use some of it to make household idols – so another of God's commands had come to be broken. Not only idols, but a graven and a molten image along with a shrine and an ephod. At this time one of his own sons was acting as the family priest. This was all far removed from what the young Levite knew well as being God's true way.

But suddenly the young traveller realized he was being offered a job by his host whom, by now, he'd discovered was called Micah. Would he like to lodge here permanently and take over from Micah's son? From Micah's point of view, it seemed desirable to secure the services of a trained, professional priestly assistant. So desirable in fact, that he'd make it worth the young man's while. Not only would he receive daily provisions, but there was a salary on offer which extended to 10 pieces of silver annually with a new suit of clothes each year thrown in.

That seemed good to the young man, and he accepted the deal. Not only would this be a new challenge, a refreshing change, it'd allow him to experiment with different religious ideas, ones which weren't constrained by strict biblical requirements. He'd gain independence, free from having to comply with others. Besides that there was the attraction of new financial security, not to mention a certain status – after all there weren't likely to be other Levites around there. And so, doubtless with some considerations like those, the compromise was readily reached. The young Levite seemed to justify the move easily, despite it being shockingly different from his Bible-based background.

This story, which closely follows the narrative of Judges chapter 17, stands as a warning from a bygone age of how easy it is in any generation to rationalize a departure from biblical teaching. The young Levite whose adventure we've been following sold out his principles big-time for 10 pieces of silver and a new suit of clothes. We rush to criticize him, but how different are we?

James Patterson and Peter Kim wrote a book entitled *The Day America Told the Truth*. In their book they asked the question, "What are you willing to do for $10,000,000?" They polled a number of Americans to see if they would agree to any of the following in return for receiving $10,000,000. Here is what they found:

25% would abandon their entire family for 10 million dollars.

25% would abandon their church for 10 million dollars.

23% would become prostitutes for a week or more in exchange for 10 million dollars.

16% would give up their American citizenship for 10 million dollars.

16% would leave their spouses for 10 million dollars.

10% would withhold testimony and let a murderer go free for 10 million dollars.

7% would murder a stranger for 10 million dollars.

3% would put their children up for adoption for 10 million dollars.

Two-thirds of all Americans polled would agree to at least one of the conditions for $10,000,000. What would you be willing to do for $10,000,000? Hopefully, you would be among the one-third who would refuse to sell their integrity. The Bible proverb gives us timeless wisdom when it counsels us to "buy truth, and do not sell it" (Proverbs 23:23). We, too, like the young man we began considering, might be tempted to experiment, to try something new, more up-to-date, more 'with-it', more seemingly rewarding and successful. It may not be financial inducement, or anything we'd recognize as status-seeking, that draws us to compromise previously held convictions, but perhaps we're rationalizing motivation that's in effect worth little more than 10 silver coins and a new suit. Don't sell the truth at any price, is the Bible's clear warning.

Let's come now to the sequel to the story we've shared so far. It's very revealing as to the apostasy of an entire tribe of Israel, and concerning the surprising identity of the Levite whom we've already featured. This is what happened next:

> "So the sons of Dan ... took what Micah had made and the priest who had belonged to him, and came to Laish,

to a people quiet and secure, and struck them with the edge of the sword; and they burned the city with fire. ... And they rebuilt the city and lived in it. They called the name of the city Dan, after the name of Dan their father who was born in Israel; however, the name of the city formerly was Laish. The sons of Dan set up for themselves the graven image; and Jonathan, the son of Gershom, the son of Manasseh, he and his sons were priests to the tribe of the Danites until the day of the captivity of the land. So they set up for themselves Micah's graven image which he had made, all the time that the house of God was at Shiloh" (Judges 18:26,28-31).

These nomadic Danites were looking for a place to settle, and here they found it, establishing a tribal centre of idolatrous worship under the priesthood of the young Levite. Perhaps, he was content to be conscripted by the Danites, seeing it as something of a promotion – now that he'd have the status of being priest to an entire tribe among his people. But we can't talk about success here. This is nothing but serious failure, and it extended through until the time of the captivity of the land - either an Assyrian captivity (for example, of Israel in 722 BC as per 2 Kings 17:6, or of the Galilean population under Tiglath-Pileser III in 733 BC - 732 BC as per 2 Kings 15:29) or an earlier unknown captivity or perhaps even it's a reference to the Philistine capture of the ark (1 Samuel 4:11). In any case, the reference to the house of God in Shiloh implies that the worship at the Danite shrine opposed the true worship of the Lord there (cf. Joshua 18:1), and this false worship in Dan became a forerunner of that of Jeroboam I who later established a Northern Kingdom shrine at Dan (cf. 1 Kings 12:28-31).

Finally, at the end of this long, intriguing chapter, the young Levite is named as Jonathan son of Gershom (cf. Exodus 2:22). The Hebrew text has inserted a (superlinear) 'n' into the name of Moses (mošeh) to make it read "Manasseh" (menasseh). One assumes this was a loyal scribe's attempt to relieve Moses' grandson, Jonathan, of involvement with idolatry. Well might he try to do that, sensing the shame this act of his grandson would bring to Moses. What had gone wrong? Was it the mixed messages from Jonathan's grandparents that led to his openness to experiment? His grandmother, Zipporah, was a Midianite, one who worshiped the moon god, and she may have been well into it initially, given that her father was a priest. When parents aren't completely united in their religious understanding, surely this uncertainty cannot fail to be transmitted – even in subtle ways. Might this then have been what contributed to Jonathan's commitment being able to be readily dissolved for a mere 10 silver coins and a suit of clothes? His tragic legacy was to be an opposition to Shiloh at very least until the Philistine conquest - and a foretaste of worse times to come under Jeroboam I – surely a legacy no grandfather would want for their grandson, especially not a grandfather of the calibre of Moses.

CHAPTER FOUR: THE GRANDSON WHO WASN'T JUDGED BECAUSE OF WHO HIS GRANDFATHER WAS

LaGuardia, mayor of New York City during the worst days of the Great Depression and all of World War II, was called 'the Little Flower' by adoring New Yorkers because he was only five foot four and always wore a carnation in his lapel. A colourful character he certainly was, and on one cold night in January of 1935, he turned up unannounced at a night court that served the poorest ward of the city, dismissed the judge for the evening, and took over the bench himself.

Within a few minutes, a tattered old woman was brought before him, charged with stealing a loaf of bread. She told LaGuardia that her daughter's husband had deserted her, her daughter was sick, and her two grandchildren were starving. But the shopkeeper, from whom the bread was stolen, refused to drop the charges. 'It's a real bad neighborhood, your Honour,' the man told the mayor. 'She's got to be punished to teach other people around here a lesson.' LaGuardia sighed. He turned to the woman and said 'I've got to punish you. The law makes no exceptions - ten dollars or ten days in jail.' But even as he pronounced sentence, the mayor was already reaching into his pocket. He extracted a bill and tossed it into his famous sombrero saying: 'Here is the ten dollar fine which I now remit; and furthermore I am going to fine everyone in this courtroom fifty cents for living in a town where a person has to steal bread so that her grandchildren can eat. Mr. Bailiff, collect the fines and give them to the defendant.'

So, the following day, the New York City newspapers reported that $47.50 was turned over to a bewildered old lady who had stolen a loaf of bread to feed her starving grandchildren; fifty cents of that amount was contributed by the red-faced grocery store owner, while some seventy petty criminals, people with traffic violations, and New York City policemen, each of whom had just paid fifty cents for the privilege of doing so, gave the mayor a standing ovation.

Our grandparent story in this chapter is a story about that kind of grace. Mephibosheth was someone who had known a life of hardship and suffering. When only 5 years old, he'd received word that he'd lost both father and grandfather in a single fateful day. Not only that, but he'd every reason to believe that he was the new king's enemy, and the next one to be killed. You see, his grandfather, Saul, had been the previous king. And often the practice then in the Middle East was that the new heir to the throne would take the entire family of the displaced king and have them put to death, to eliminate the possibility of any future opposition and rebellion – and, remember, Mephibosheth was a grandson of the previous king. So, it's entirely possible that he lived in fear, dreading the day a knock would come to his door.

He'd previously seen his grandfather go practically insane, losing control both of himself and his kingdom. Following the news he'd received on that fateful day we mentioned a moment ago, he'd no father to guide him and no grandfather to shower him with love and affection. But there's more to his story, and more pain, I'm afraid. Imagine the pain of remembering being in the arms of someone you specially trusted, and running for your life. Such had been Mephibosheth, fleeing with his nurse, when they'd brought the news of the death of his father and grandfather. Then, on the rocky hill paths, the nurse had slipped and dropped him (2 Samuel 4:4). He'd come crashing down on his feet, and severe pain overwhelmed him in an instant. I guess both his feet were broken. But there was no time to get him to a doctor – or anyone who might have been able to set the bones correctly. They had to think about survival. So, the nurse picked him up and continued to carry him. As a result, the bones never mended correctly. He was left crippled, living in obscurity and poverty in a remote and barren corner of the kingdom.

Mephibosheth may also have lived with increasing fear for his own life, because David was getting stronger as king; on the other hand, Mephibosheth's family was getting weaker. Any day he might receive a knock on the door and be taken away to be executed or tortured. His uncle, Ishbosheth, was killed. Mephibosheth might have wondered, "Will I be next?" Then one day, it happened. There came that knock on the door that he dreaded (2 Samuel 9:5). He was summoned to appear before king David. Mephibosheth knew nothing of David's intent, he could only expect the worst. All that he knew was a servant, Ziba, who knew where he was living came and told him that he was to be taken to the king's palace. Well, I guess he hobbled into the throne room of the powerful king. I'm not sure he'd have known that David, the king, had been a great friend of his father, Jonathan. In which case, when he appeared before David, he could have be forgiven for thinking, 'I'm going to be killed because Saul was my grandfather – the very man who had insanely tried to kill this present king!'

Mephibosheth fell on his face, and he heard the king speak his name – 'Mephibosheth!' (2 Samuel 9:6). We might wonder if David saw any resemblance of his friend, Jonathan, on his son Mephibosheth's face: the same look in his eyes perhaps; the same expressive face; perhaps some of the same mannerisms. "Don't be afraid," David said to him, "since I intend to show you kindness because of your father Jonathan. I will restore to you all your grandfather Saul's fields, and you will always eat meals at my table'" (2 Samuel 9:7). This was unbelievable grace. How did Mephibosheth respond? He said: "What is your servant, that you should notice a dead dog like me?" (v.8). Could it be that way of referring to himself echoed the disdain he'd become accustomed to? After all, he was crippled; an outcast; a dead dog. But David never used those terms – far from it.

Words have a way of changing us, don't they? I once heard about an employer in the United States back in the days when black Americans were segregated. This man refused to stay in a motel because they wouldn't allow his black assistant to lodge with him. Instead, they both slept in the boss' van in the parking lot. The boss had told the motel manager that this black employee was like family to him. Later, that same employee would testify that the description of him as 'family' changed his life – because his white boss had said he was like family to him.

David's words changed Mephibosheth's life, too. Words have a powerful way of bringing healing and restoration. A kind word can restore a person's dignity. The kindness Mephibosheth received from the king was overwhelming. David's love for him because of the faithfulness and loyalty of his father, Jonathan, was an unexpected, unanticipated joy. He was still lame, of course, but no longer with a questionable future - now he was sitting at the king's table, as one of his own sons. David's words were not just a token gesture; they were extravagant - symbolic of his love for Jonathan. His words expressed grace – a reflection of God's love for David. His love, too, was a demonstration of love toward a man who didn't deserve it, and could never earn it, and would never be able to repay it. David, the strong and famous king, reached out to Mephibosheth, the cripple and outcast, and expressed kindness to him such as he had never known before.

To eat at the king's table was not a temporary honour; it was like drawing a pension from the king for the rest of his life. David's kindness would continue throughout Mephibosheth's life. The 'dead dog' knew the wonderful feeling of acceptance; the joy of being drawn into a family; the warmth of love; the contentment that comes when someone cares. Do we tend to stay away from the Mephibosheth's of the world - the crippled, the handicapped, and the marginalized; avoiding the Downs Syndrome boy because of embarrassment? All people matter to God. David restored Mephibosheth from a place in the wilderness to a place at his table. From a place of barrenness to a place of honour. From a place with no pasture ('Lo-debar,' v.4) to a place of plenty.

When David had originally asked, "Is there anyone left of Saul's family I can show the kindness of God to?" (2 Samuel 9:3), the word for kindness is the biblical word 'hesed.' It means 'lovingkindness'. God had demonstrated grace and kindness to David in so many ways. His life had been spared on numerous occasions. Now, David wanted to reciprocate that kindness. Those who have been touched by the grace of God surely want to pass it on. What David did for Mephibosheth, God does for us. Just as the king brought the outcast into the palace and made him a son, God adopts us into his family. Let's enjoy that thought as we reflect in conclusion on Paul's famous eulogy:

> "Blessed be the God and Father of our Lord Jesus Christ, who has blessed us with every spiritual blessing in the heavenly places in Christ, just as He chose us in Him before the foundation of the world, that we would be holy and blameless before Him. In love He predestined us to adoption as sons through Jesus Christ to Himself, according to the kind intention of His will, to the praise of the glory of His grace, which He freely bestowed on us in the Beloved. In Him we have

redemption through His blood, the forgiveness of our trespasses, according to the riches of His grace which He lavished on us" (Ephesians 1:3-8).

Now let's pass it on by showing grace to others we meet!

CHAPTER FIVE: HOW A FOREIGNER BECAME (GREAT) GRANDMOTHER TO KING DAVID

During a time of famine, an Israelite family take matters into their own hands and exit from the land of God's promise. Perhaps they lived in the land of Moab longer than they originally intended; it was certainly long enough for their two sons to find wives there. But tragedy struck, and all the menfolk died leaving Naomi and her two daughters-in-law, one of whom was called Ruth. Much later, Naomi hears there is food once again in their homeland, so they finally head back. At the end of chapter 1 of the book of Ruth, Naomi appears to be in 'meltdown.' Try to pick up on five complaints she expresses regarding God's dealings with her. She says:

> "... the hand of the LORD has gone forth against me.' ... And when they had come to Bethlehem, all the city was stirred because of them, and the women said, "Is this Naomi?" She said to them, "Do not call me Naomi; call me Mara, for the Almighty has dealt very bitterly with me. "I went out full, but the LORD has brought me back empty. Why do you call me Naomi, since the LORD has witnessed against me and the Almighty has afflicted me?" (Ruth 1:13,19-21).

On the other hand, Ruth's reply to her mother-in-law who has tried to persuade her to remain behind in Moab, is as follows – try to listen out for five affirmations Ruth gives to Naomi:

"But Ruth said, "Do not urge me to leave you or turn back from following you; for where you go, I will go, and where you lodge, I will lodge. Your people shall be my people, and your God, my God. "Where you die, I will die, and there I will be buried. Thus may the LORD do to me, and worse, if anything but death parts you and me." (Ruth 1:16-17).

We'll come back to this point, but it's worth reflecting on whether there are lessons we can draw for our own times of adversity? How can we be like Ruth, and not like Naomi? Specifically, how can we avoid becoming bitter, as Naomi freely confesses herself to be? But let's leave that thought hanging for the moment, and continue to focus purely on the information we can pick up from the first two chapters – and for the moment ignoring the ending of the story we know so well – I want to ask you what, do you think, is the ending that we are being led to expect up until this point?

In chapter 1, Naomi is determined to return alone. If that's the case, must she not have assumed she'd be the one to remarry and so provide an heir for the family land to remain in their possession? She even talks that way when she says: "if I should even have a husband tonight ..." (1:12). I think we can assume that Naomi was still of child-bearing age. Next, consider the clue in the first verse of the second chapter. It's there we're told: "Naomi had a kinsman of her husband, a man of great wealth, of the family of Elimelech, whose name was Boaz" (Ruth 2:1).

Notice, of course, he's described as Naomi's kinsman or relative. This was a meaningful way of referring to Boaz under the provisions of the Old Testament law for God's people. If you fell into financial difficulty back in those days, you could appeal for help from a close relative. This person if they were the one to help you, would become known as your 'kinsman redeemer.' To redeem means to buy back, as from a pawn shop. It was this person's expected family duty to buy land that you were being forced to sell due to hardship. It was also lawful for such a man to marry his brother's widow to raise up those of the next generation who would own and farm the land. Land in Israel was kept in the tribal families in this way. But the point here is Boaz is Naomi's kinsman. We are being prepared for him to fulfil his duty towards Naomi. This is because the first verse chooses to shine a spotlight on Naomi and who Boaz was in relation to her.

However, Ruth is the one to go out to work on behalf of her mother-in-law and herself. It turns out that she ends up in a field belonging to Boaz who is harvesting his crops. Poor people in those days were allowed to help themselves to any leftovers. Boaz notices her and enquires who she is; only to be told by the servant in charge of the reapers: "She is the young Moabite woman who returned with Naomi from the land of Moab" (Ruth 2:6). Boaz was well-informed and was already up to speed concerning Naomi's circumstances. He shares this in conversation with Ruth: "Boaz replied to her, 'All that you have done for your mother-in-law after the death of your husband has been fully reported to me, and how you left your father and your mother and the land of your birth, and came to a people that you did not previously know" (Ruth 2:11).

Still, in everything Boaz says, his focus and reference point is Naomi, his relative. After all, the younger woman, Ruth, is a stranger to him. A careful reader quickly notices that while Boaz certainly appreciated Ruth's sterling qualities, his heart tended more to Naomi. Naomi was, after all, his kin, the wife of his relative, a part of his world and his heritage. According to the plain sense of the verses, Naomi was still fertile and not much older than Ruth, perhaps in her mid-thirties (see 1:12-13). Even if Naomi was older, she was a more fitting partner for the twilight of Boaz's life. Some might say that Naomi was a natural; but Ruth was a gamble. In any case, we find that Boaz appreciated and praised Ruth for what she has done for Naomi.

When Ruth returns home in the evening, with food for them both, Naomi asks how she had got on, and in whose field she'd ended up working. Ruth explains, to which Naomi then replies happily: "May he be blessed of the LORD who has not withdrawn his kindness to the living and to the dead." Again Naomi said to her, "The man is our relative, he is one of our closest relatives" (Ruth 2:20). At the beginning of the second chapter, we've observed how the first verse uses an intentional ambiguity for it can be read as suggesting that Boaz was to be a husband for Naomi. If so, we might expect Naomi to reach out to Boaz but she does not. Instead – and here comes the twist in the tale – Naomi prepares Ruth to present herself to Boaz as a claimant for the right of being redeemed. In effect, it was a proposal of marriage.

"And Naomi her mother-in-law said unto her: 'My daughter, shall I not seek security for you, that it may be well with you? Now is not Boaz our kinsman ..." (Ruth 3:1-2). It's all handled in a rather secretive or hush-hush way. And that's my point again. For if it was expected or natural that Ruth would be the proposer, why the furtiveness of chapter 3? Something intriguing is happening here. Providence led her to him, but Naomi assisted. I just want to pause and say that the book of Ruth is not really the romantic storyline that it's often made out to be. These are business transactions, in effect. And it's quite unexpected when Ruth is ushered into the frame in Naomi's place. Why the twist in the tail of the tale? Naomi was still fertile (1:13) we assume, a better match by age for Boaz, closer to the situation of Deuteronomy 25:5, and the actual owner of the field - so why is Ruth seen as more appropriate?

It has to be said that even Naomi, who self-sacrificingly puts her forward to great honour (Matthew 1:5), appears to see Ruth as the more appropriate person. Why does Naomi do this? Might it be that Naomi has come to see Ruth as a more worthy person than herself? We began by highlighting the contrast between Naomi's bitter complaints regarding God's dealings with her – over against the very virtuous and positive commitment Ruth makes to Naomi. Ruth is described in the book as a virtuous woman, a woman of some substance.

The focus abruptly shifts to Ruth. Even at the point that Boaz commits to Ruth, he's still thinking of Naomi: And she said: "These six measures of barley he gave me; for he said to me: Go not empty unto your mother-in-law" (Ruth 3:17). Naomi could have had Boaz but in an act of profound selflessness she put Ruth forward instead. Why did Naomi do this? Was it simply the sense of gratitude and obligation that the older woman felt for the younger one, her who left her people and her land to share Naomi's fate? Or, was it that she felt Ruth was more suited to play the role that history had prepared for Boaz? Naomi knew Ruth and she understood Boaz - for Ruth and Boaz shared a quality that perhaps Naomi herself felt she no longer possessed. Significantly Boaz describes Ruth with the same words that the verse describes him. Boaz is a man of valour and Ruth is a woman of valour (Ruth 3:11).

But, we ask, is Naomi not a closer relative for triggering the marriage custom of those times? Is she not the actual owner of the field that Boaz is supposed to redeem? Is she not one who should have more fittingly given birth to a messianic king than Ruth, the stranger, the Moabite? Why the switchover? We must ask to what purpose did Scripture recount Naomi's 'breakdown' upon return to Bethlehem. On the surface, it contributes little to the story. In truth, however, it's essential. Yes, Naomi would have been perfect for Boaz. But, in a sense, Naomi no longer existed. In her place, by her own testimony, there now stood another woman, weighed down by suffering, embittered and not at peace with God, a woman called Marah. On the other hand, Ruth has dedicated herself to the God whom she knew only as one who'd taken her husband away and withheld children from her womb. David and the Jewish people needed an ancestor such as this. Did Boaz, Naomi and Ruth understand that Ruth was suited to be a mother of Obed, the grandfather of King David, in a way that Naomi could no longer be?

CHAPTER SIX: A GRANDSON WHO PROVED A WORTHY SUCCESSOR TO HIS GRANDFATHER

There's a time to speak and a time to keep silent (Ecclesiastes 3:1). Aaron, Israel's first ever high priest, knew that. He and his four sons had the remarkable honour of drawing near before God as they officiated in the people's worship. It was a privilege that others envied (Numbers 16). But such proximity to the holy God spelt danger to any who were tempted to be disobedient.

> "Now Nadab and Abihu, the sons of Aaron, took their respective firepans, and after putting fire in them, placed incense on it and offered strange fire before the LORD, which He had not commanded them. And fire came out from the presence of the LORD and consumed them, and they died before the LORD. Then Moses said to Aaron, "It is what the LORD spoke, saying, 'By those who come near Me I will be treated as holy, And before all the people I will be honoured.' So Aaron, therefore, kept silent" (Leviticus 10:1-3).

Isn't that remarkable? His two sons had been burned to a crisp in the presence of God. Their ill-fated attempt at some form of alternative worship had drawn God's anger. This is the anger of God that burns against sin, and departures from God's instructions are always sin. The Bible warns us that the God we serve is a consuming fire. He's the same today. How do we react to this incident? With a sense of shock, horror or disbelief? If that's the case, we've still a long way to go in becoming truly sanctified.

When one coming day we stand with Christ in glory, and we're then glorified in him - at that time when our Christ-likeness is complete - then we'll fully understand this incident (and any others like it which tend to trouble us now when we read God's Word).

But notice Aaron's reaction back then. Remember, his two sons have just been struck down dead. Moses' commentary on what's just happened is to tell his brother that his two sons hadn't treated God as holy and so they'd not honoured him before all the congregation. That's straight-talking which might sound to our ears today as being rather short on brotherly compassion. But what did Aaron reply? Did you pick up on it? Yes, Aaron kept silent. That's extraordinary, wouldn't you agree? It was then that Moses went on to add that the father and brothers of the deceased were not even allowed to mourn their loss. However, alternative provision was to be made ...

> "Moses called also to Mishael and Elzaphan, the sons of Aaron's uncle Uzziel, and said to them, "Come forward, carry your relatives away from the front of the sanctuary to the outside of the camp." So they came forward and carried them still in their tunics to the outside of the camp, as Moses had said. Then Moses said to Aaron and to his sons Eleazar and Ithamar, "Do not uncover your heads nor tear your clothes, so that you will not die and that [the LORD] will not become wrathful against all the congregation. But your kinsmen, the whole house of Israel, shall bewail the burning which the LORD has brought about" (Leviticus 10:4-6).

How guarded we should be today when someone we know sins against the Lord. It may be that they have 'only' done something that's now commonplace in the world. We no longer expect them to face the summary judgement of God, but God's actions back then indicate what his attitude is today. For God doesn't change (see Malachi 3:6). Beware of the fact that the world's opinion of fairness is usually well wide of the mark. Serious offences in God's estimation are dismissed as mere 'indiscretions' or 'lapses of judgement' by the world. Sometimes, in the view of society, you have to do wrong in order to do right. We can get carried away in such a way of thinking – simply because it faces us on every side – to the point that people end up celebrating what the Bible describes as a sinful act. When God expresses himself in judgement – either by action or usually today by a statement found in his Word, the Bible – it's not for us to mourn, far less to celebrate with those who are culpable. We are in every bit as much need to learn the fear of the Lord and how to treat him as holy in a profane worldly environment.

The story of the frog put into a pan of water which is being slowly heated is a salutary one. The frog's body is able to adjust to compensate for the rising water temperature. But then the water is all of a sudden too hot, and the frog dies. We can so easily find ourselves in a similar type of danger. We can easily become desensitized to God's holy standards by the spirit of the times in which we live. If we allow ourselves to become immersed in the surrounding culture, we too can find our standards being eroded. In practice, this might mean that we tolerate watching movies which our parents would not have tolerated – or even which we ourselves would not have judged acceptable a few years earlier. What's happening? We are acclimatizing ourselves to what the world finds acceptable. Imperceptibly, but gradually, our sensitivity to what displeases the Lord is being eroded.

Let's return to where we left Aaron silently mourning the loss of two of his sons, struck down in a moment by the holy anger of God. That left him with only two remaining sons, Eleazar and

Ithamar, to carry on the line of the high priest after him. Eleazar is mentioned first, but for reasons which aren't explained to us, the office of high priest seemed at some point to pass to the line of Ithamar. It was so in the days of the old priest Eli at the beginning of First Samuel. But Eli honoured his sons more than he honoured God, and God announced that the line of descent would be switched back again – which is what happened when Solomon succeeded his father David as king and appointed Zadok the priest in place of Abiathar (1 Kings 1). This was the outworking of the clear principle which God had first sounded to Eli: that whoever honours God will be honoured by God.

Aaron, then, had known personal failings, and severe disappointment in his priestly family, but in his grandson Phineas, the son of Eleazar, he would have a distinguished successor. If we dip into the Bible book of Numbers, we can find an inspiring account of Phineas' passion for the honour of God at a very black time in Israel's chequered history:

> "Israel ... began to play the harlot with the daughters of Moab. For they invited the people to the sacrifices of their gods, and the people ate and bowed down to their gods. So Israel joined themselves to Baal of Peor, and the LORD was angry against Israel. The LORD said to Moses, "Take all the leaders of the people and execute them in broad daylight before the LORD, so that the fierce anger of the LORD may turn away from Israel." So Moses said to the judges of Israel, "Each of you slay his men who have joined themselves to Baal of Peor." Then behold, one of the sons of Israel came and brought to his relatives a Midianite woman, in the sight of Moses and in the sight of all the congregation of the sons of Israel, while they were weeping at the doorway of the tent of meeting. When Phinehas the son of Eleazar, the

son of Aaron the priest, saw it, he arose from the midst of the congregation and took a spear in his hand, and he went after the man of Israel into the tent and pierced both of them through, the man of Israel and the woman, through the body. So the plague on the sons of Israel was checked. Those who died by the plague were 24,000.

Then the LORD spoke to Moses, saying, "Phinehas the son of Eleazar, the son of Aaron the priest, has turned away My wrath from the sons of Israel in that he was jealous with My jealousy among them, so that I did not destroy the sons of Israel in My jealousy. "Therefore say, 'Behold, I give him My covenant of peace; and it shall be for him and his descendants after him, a covenant of a perpetual priesthood, because he was jealous for his God and made atonement for the sons of Israel" (Numbers 25:1-13).

Those are remarkable words – that Phineas was jealous with God's own jealousy. Jealousy gets a bad press, and often it is very rightly an undesirable trait. But it does depend on the circumstances. It would be wrong for any husband not to be jealous if another man became a rival for his wife's affections. God's relationship with the people of Israel in Old Testament times was pictured in that way – by analogy with a marriage. When Israel went after the gods of the surrounding nations, they were acting unfaithfully with respect to the true God who loved them better than any husband has ever loved his wife. Phineas, the priest, was someone who had a clear glimpse of God's holy love for his people, and he was jealous on God's behalf when his compatriots were flagrantly unfaithful to God. How does this affect us? We come to Paul's words to the Church of God at Corinth:

> "For I am jealous for you with a godly jealousy; for I betrothed you to one husband, so that to Christ I might present you as a pure virgin. But I am afraid that, as the serpent deceived Eve by his craftiness, your minds will be led astray from the simplicity and purity of devotion to Christ. For if one comes and preaches another Jesus whom we have not preached, or you receive a different spirit which you have not received, or a different gospel which you have not accepted, you bear this beautifully" (2 Corinthians 11:2-4).

Like Phineas, Paul the apostle was jealous with a jealousy like God's own. The Apostle's jealousy was stirred by the readiness of the Christians at Corinth to become doctrinally impure, even to the extent of embracing a totally false Gospel. Paul both visited and wrote to them to apply correction. And later, the second Bible letter he wrote to them shows that when Paul later tested the Church at Corinth (compare the test of a potentially unfaithful wife detailed in Numbers chapter 5), they passed the test of faithfulness. May we do also!

CHAPTER SEVEN: THE GRANDMOTHER WHO TEAMED UP TO RAISE A MAN OF GOD

Lots of grandmothers are mentioned in the Bible, but Second Timothy is the only place where the term 'grandmother' is actually used – and it's to tell us about someone called Lois:

> "Paul, ... To Timothy, my beloved son: Grace, mercy and peace from God the Father and Christ Jesus our Lord ... I constantly remember you in my prayers night and day, longing to see you, even as I recall your tears, so that I may be filled with joy. For I am mindful of the sincere faith within you, which first dwelt in your grandmother Lois and your mother Eunice, and I am sure that it is in you as well" (2 Timothy 1:1,4-5).

Lois was a devout Jewess who had obviously instructed her daughter and grandson in the Old Testament Scriptures. We know nothing at all about her husband, but we do know that their daughter was given a Greek name, which might indicate that the father, Lois' husband, was also a Greek. The family lived in Lystra, among a people who worshipped the gods of Greece, but somehow Lois succeeded in raising a daughter who loved the God of the Bible. The Apostle Paul came in to their lives as follows:

> "Paul came ... to Lystra. And a disciple was there, named Timothy, the son of a Jewish woman who was a believer, but his father was a Greek, and he was well spoken of by the brethren who were in Lystra and Iconium. Paul

wanted this man to go with him; and he took him and circumcised him because of the Jews who were in those parts, for they all knew that his father was a Greek" (Acts 16:1-3).

Eunice, that Jewish woman in question, and daughter of Lois, lived up to her name which means 'conquering well' - inasmuch as she too had gained the victory over that same pagan society by raising a God-fearing son. She'd also had married a Greek man, a Gentile, and presumably an unbeliever. They had a son, Timothy. Nothing else is said about Timothy's father, so we may be correct in assuming he was dead by the time his wife Eunice met the Apostle Paul – at which point they feature in the New Testament story. How Eunice, the daughter of the pious Lois, had come to marry a pagan Greek, we don't know. And equally, we don't know of the circumstances which led the family to settle at Lystra (Acts 16:1; compare 14:6, etc.), a place where there wasn't even a Jewish synagogue.

That fact could well imply that at most two or three Jewish families lived there. Perhaps Lois and Eunice were the only worshippers of the God of Abraham living there; for we don't even read of a meeting-place for prayer, such as the one down by the river-side where Paul first met Lydia. Yet in such adverse circumstances, and as the wife of a Greek, Eunice proved to be someone to whom royal Lemuel's praise applied in the fullest sense: "Her children arise up and call her blessed," and "Her works praise her in the gates" – where we might well be thinking of the gates of the new Jerusalem.

Just to recap, there was no synagogue in Lystra where Timothy might have heard Moses and the Prophets read every Sabbath. There was little conducive religious companionship available nor the means for instruction of any kind, nor even a father's example.

In a house like that of Timothy's father, there would, of course, be no 'mezuzas' – those little containers of portions of Scripture which Jewish homes had attached to the doorposts. But we know that from the time of the Syrian persecutions, just before the uprising of the Maccabees, portions of the Old Testament were quite often owned by private families – at least in Israel. It seems this was the means of instruction at the disposal of Eunice for teaching her son.

Early in Bible history, God let his thoughts be known concerning Abraham, the father of the Jews, saying: "I know him, that he will command his children ... after him" (Genesis 18:19). It seems then that Eunice, and her mother Lois before her, were true daughters of Abraham. Indeed, they were both such as could be described as virtuous women – to quote from how the Book of Proverbs ends. And that book contains the fullest appreciation of women in their true dignity, especially in the early upbringing of children. In fact, the two last chapters of the book of Proverbs introduce to us the royal family of Massa (an area beyond the limits of the Holy Land, close by Dumah, see Genesis 25:14), as a family deeply saturated with the spiritual religion of the Old Testament – to the extent that in Proverbs 31:1 we find the mother of the heir to the throne training her son in the knowledge and fear of the Lord (the word 'prophecy,' Proverbs 30:1; 31:1 KJV, is simply the name of a district - 'Massa') – not only that but her maternal instruction is actually captured as part of the inspired record of the Old Testament!

Well, back to Lois and Eunice. There's no doubt that their devout Jewish faith and knowledge of the Old Testament Scriptures had prepared their hearts to receive the words of Paul regarding eternal life through Jesus Christ – which is of course what God had designed those Old Testament Scriptures to do. Paul speaks of the unfeigned faith that was in Timothy, and he adds that this faith dwelt at the first in his grandmother Lois, and his mother Eunice.

Timothy hadn't been circumcised in childhood, probably due to his father's Gentile influence; but mother and grandmother certainly did all in their power to train Timothy in the fear of God and in the knowledge of the Old Testament Scriptures. His careful home training led to him being prepared to give a welcome both to Paul and to the gospel proclaimed by him, when the apostle in his first great missionary journey came to Lystra, one of the cities of Lycaonia or Southern Galatia, where Eunice and her family lived. This is implied in the account of Paul's second missionary journey (Acts 16:1), where we read that he came to Lystra, and found there a certain disciple named Timothy, the son of a certain woman who was a Jewess, who believed. It's clear that Eunice and Timothy were not brought to a knowledge of the gospel at this time, but that they were already Christians; she, 'a believer'; he, 'a disciple.' This evidently means that Eunice, Lois and Timothy had been converted on Paul's former visit to Lystra.

This conclusion is confirmed in 2 Timothy 3:11, where Paul recalls to Timothy the fact that he had fully known the persecutions and afflictions which came to him at Lystra. These persecutions happened on Paul's first visit to that city. Eunice was therefore one of those who on that occasion became disciples. And her faith in Christ, and her son's faith too, were genuine, and stood the test of 'much tribulation' which Paul had warned them about (Acts 14:22). On his second missionary tour, Paul found the young man highly spoken of by the little group of Christians in that city. He was of such evident ability and promise that Paul made him a missionary helper. Eunice lived up to her name for she conquered in the effort to bring up her son in the nurture and admonition of the Lord, such that he became a famous evangelist. Years later, when Paul lay in the prison at Rome awaiting trial and likely execution, he writes his second letter to his beloved helper, nostalgically reminiscing over the faith Timothy had shown, and reminding him that this same faith was first in his grandmother Lois and his mother Eunice.

As Paul prayed for Timothy night and day, his gratitude for Timothy kept welling up anew. Sitting chained in a Roman prison there was little else Paul could do but pray; and Timothy, perhaps Paul's closest companion, ministering to the church that Paul probably knew best, was no doubt the single most common focus of his prayers. Paul remembered Timothy's tears on their last parting, possibly at Paul's second Roman arrest. In this last ever Bible letter, he would ask Timothy to join him in Rome (cf. 4:9,21). Paul had longed for Timothy's companionship which was such a joy to him. Even the great apostle at times became lonely, discouraged, and in need of support from fellow Christians.

So many, it seems, had opposed or deserted Paul (cf. 1:15; 2:17; 3:1-9,13; 4:3-4,10-21) that Timothy's sincere faith stood out in bold relief. Paul attributed Timothy's faith to the influence of his Jewish mother Eunice and grandmother Lois. If, according to this verse, Paul seems rather to attribute Timothy's conversion to his mother and grandmother (cf. 2 Timothy 3:15), it must then mean that references to Timothy as Paul's son in the faith (cf. 1:2; 2:1; 1 Timothy 1:2) should be understood to mean a mentor-protégé relationship.

The name Timothy means 'someone who fears God', a name obviously picked by his faithful mother. The record of Timothy demonstrates the value of positive Christian training in the home. Lois and Eunice took the responsibility to pass on their faith very seriously and as a result they raised up a young man who became a servant of Christ. For this, they've gone down in history as outstanding mothers and great women of faith. The striking feature of the Scriptural record of Eunice and Lois is their spiritual

Jewish influence on Timothy. It was from them also that he derived his first impressions of Christian truth; for Paul calls to remembrance the earnest faith which first dwelt in them. How gratified they must have been when Timothy set out to do the work of an evangelist (2 Timothy 4:5)!

After Paul's reference to Lois and Eunice in his second epistle to Timothy, they're not mentioned again. The important thing we pick up from the little we read about them concerns the value of positive Christian training in the home. This is an encouragement to all mothers who want to raise their children to love God. Lois and Eunice were a mother/daughter team that raised up a man of God. These women were responsible for passing their faith on to the next generation. His fitness to be the companion and co-worker of Paul finds its explanation largely in the home training and pious example given him by these two noble women.

CHAPTER EIGHT: THE GRANDMOTHER WHO HELPED A CURSE BECOME A BLESSING

We've all heard the kind of simple puzzle that asks: Sally's mother had three daughters. The first two were called April and May. What, do you think, was the name of the third? Ah, of course, far too easy for you! But today, I've got something just a little more taxing. Please don't be put off, because it really does showcase superbly how God's mercy triumphs over his judgement. It also explains how God's son can one day sit on king David's throne. What we have to share in this final chapter is the remarkable story of a grandmother who played a pivotal role in God's plans for the Messiah. Her remarkable and strategic contribution was borne out of recurring sadness and, also remarkably, we're never told her name, only that she was the daughter of someone called Neri. Now, any guesses as to who Neri's great-grandson was? He was a man greatly blessed by the Lord. That's a harder puzzle, perhaps, but all will soon be revealed.

First, I'd like to point out a common link between Joseph's genealogy which we get in Matthew chapter 1, and Mary's genealogy which is listed in Luke's Gospel, chapter 3. Here's the Matthew reading first:

> "Josiah became the father of Jeconiah and his brothers, at the time of the deportation to Babylon. After the deportation to Babylon: Jeconiah became the father of Shealtiel, and Shealtiel the father of Zerubbabel.

Zerubbabel was the father of Abihud ..." (Matthew 1:11-13).

And now from Luke 3:27, we have:

"... the son of Joanan, the son of Rhesa, the son of Zerubbabel, the son of Shealtiel, the son of Neri."

Hopefully, you noticed the overlap there, given away by the repeated names of Shealtiel and Zerubbabel. And, if that name is ringing bells for you, it will be because you're already familiar with the story of the return of the Jews from their exile in Babylon and how God used prophets like Haggai to re-energise his people for the work of reconstructing the Jerusalem temple. Near to the end of the prophet Haggai's short message, we find these words: "I will take you, Zerubbabel, son of Shealtiel ... and I will make you like a signet ring" (Haggai 2:23). This was God's marvellous promise to this man, Zerubbabel, and it's at once noteworthy for the fact that it reverses an earlier curse which was pronounced in the same terms upon his grandfather, one of the last kings before the Jewish people were deported to Babylon. Here's what another prophet, the prophet Jeremiah, said:

"Even though [Je]coniah ... were a signet ring on My right hand, yet I would pull you off ... I will hurl you ... into another country ... there you will die. But as for that land to which they desire to return, they will not return to it ... write this man down childless, a man who will not prosper in his days; for no man of his descendants will prosper sitting on the throne of David or ruling again in Judah" (Jeremiah 22:24-30).

God watches over his word to perform it, and soon it was fulfilled that Jeconiah (sometimes called Coniah or Jehoiachin) was defeated by the Babylonians and taken captive to the city of Babylon. There, Jeconiah's prosperity was restored, in Babylon where he died. He did have a son by the name of Shealtiel who never reigned as a king of Israel. What's more, this man died before producing an heir. According to the promise, Jeconiah's descendants did return to Israel, from the time of his grandsons' generation. So, the royal bloodline, now under a curse, seems to have come to an end with Shealtiel. That satisfies the prophecy of Jeremiah. God's judgement had terminated the line. But when we come to the opening of the New Testament – to Matthew chapter 1 as we saw – Jeconiah is in fact listed in the royal line which does continue down to Christ. How does this not contradict the Jeremiah prophecy? It seems at first sight this is a contradiction in the Bible – and a pretty major one, as it touches on Christ's legal human right to reign in the future on David's throne.

There's a wonderful explanation for how this puzzle was solved. It involves what will likely be a strange custom to us, so let me talk you through that first of all. The Law of God through Moses had made this provision to maintain family names and keep the inheritance of land etc. within the family. This is from Deuteronomy 25:5:

> "When brothers live together and one of them dies and has no son, the wife of the deceased shall not be married outside the family to a strange man. Her husband's brother shall go in to her and take her to himself as wife and perform the duty of a husband's brother to her."

Let's recap where we've got to. The cursed king, Jeconiah – cursed for his disobedience – has been told that he'd be childless, at least childless with respect to the throne. It's important to pick up clearly on that qualification, for we've commented that Jeconiah did have a son, Shealtiel. But he never sat on the throne, so the prophecy was fulfilled, as neither did he have any natural offspring who became king. How then is it possible that this man's name can still feature in the royal line of descent which in the New Testament stretches down to Christ?

The answer is found in the fact that the king married a widow. The daughter of Neri was a widow (with a son, Pedaiah) before marrying Coniah. They then had a son together, Shealtiel, who married, but died before fathering a son. It was then incumbent – according to the law we quoted - upon Pedaiah to marry his step-brother's wife to raise up seed to his step-brother, Shealtiel. By virtue of the (by our standards) exceptional provision of the Old Testament law, Zerubbabel (and Shealtiel legally) ends up being in both Joseph and Mary's line of descent from David, and so in Christ's (via Mary only). It should be noted that Mary's bloodline was literally free of Jeconiah, but her descent was not legally clear of him – the legal aspect is important in order to establish her son's right to the throne – that is Christ's legal human right to David's throne. It is an amazing story of how, by God's overruling, the actual bloodline through Nathan and the legal right to the throne through Solomon are brought together in Zerubbabel.

Zerubbabel's name means 'born in Babylon'. Upon this man so tainted with Israel's sinful past and captivity was conferred the legal right to the throne of David. In itself this is another revelation of God's ways of grace. This special circumstance had necessarily Involved his grandmother being widowed. We can only imagine this sad event and the grief it caused at the time. Happiness seemed to return to her life with a proposal of marriage from the man who was then king. Whether this was a happy marriage we don't know, as her husband was to incur God's severe displeasure which resulted in him and his natural offspring coming under a curse – which was that neither they nor their natural descendants would ever reign as kings on David's throne.

However, in a very real sense, this must have been a marriage 'made in heaven' as it was God's gracious solution as to how David's dynasty could indeed be maintained, despite the curse effectively meaning the dynasty had come to an end. But there would first be more sadness and pain ahead for this dear lady whom we only know as 'the daughter of Neri.' For she was to suffer the tragic early death of the son she bore to the king, His name was Shealtiel as we now know, but he didn't live long enough to produce an heir.

Zerubbabel, as we can read for ourselves in the Bible books of Haggai and Zechariah, was someone who chose to obey God – and how blessed he was in his obedience! Curiously then, Zerubbabel was the result of a son's widow (his mother) marrying a widow's (his grandmother) son! The man 'born in Babylon,' born in the outside place, turned the curse of disobedience into blessing through his obedience, and became a leader of God's people and builder of God's house.

In terms of the overall story-line of the Old Testament, the Israelites have at this point returned from captivity in Babylon to rebuild the Jerusalem Temple. This project was being slowed by opposition, but God gave encouragement that the reconstruction would be completed:

> "'Not by might nor by power, but by My Spirit,' says the Lord of hosts. 'What are you, O great mountain? Before Zerubbabel you will become a plain; and he will bring forth the top stone with shouts of "Grace, grace to it!"'" Also the word of the Lord came to me, saying, "The hands of Zerubbabel have laid the foundation of this house, and his hands will finish it. Then you will know that the Lord of hosts has sent me to you. For who has despised the day of small things? But these seven will be

glad when they see the plumb line in the hand of Zerubbabel - these are the eyes of the Lord which range to and fro throughout the earth" (Zechariah 4:6-10).

The expression 'the day of small things' (Zechariah 4:10) seems to have been a disparaging term applied to the current efforts by those who longed after the past glories of this temple's more magnificent predecessor. But while they looked back, God was looking forward. In the book of Zechariah, he speaks of how his eye anticipated Zerubbabel's final checks using a plumb line, showing the temple he was building was true to God's own pattern. That was a source of gladness for God and he said so. How encouraging that must have been for the disheartened workers!

In church life, our efforts can seem so feeble, and results may be small, but when we have the assurance of the Spirit's working (v.6), we can take courage from God's different perspective as we build to his pattern. Back then, the promise was that mountainous difficulties (v.7) would be removed, and the work finished. Zerubbabel, the governor who'd begun the work, was going to finish it as well (v.9). The foundation stone had been laid by his hands, and so would the 'headstone' at the topmost elevation which completed the project. In our case, while we view Jesus, the head of the corner, as Son over God's spiritual house in churches of God today (Hebrews 3:6), let's aim to be finishers for God!

Did you love *Learning from Bible Grandparents*? Then you should read *If Atheism Is True...* by Brian Johnston!

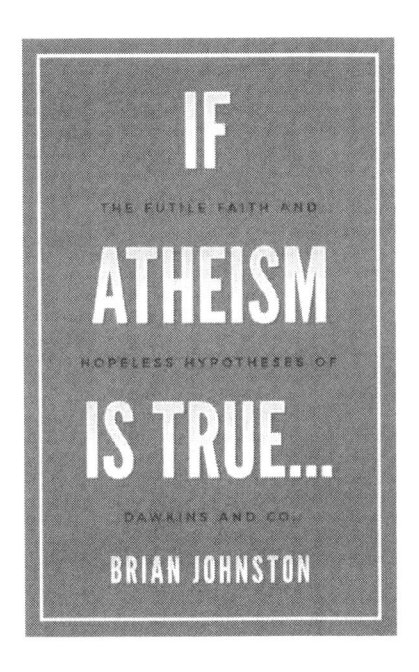

IF
THE FUTILE FAITH AND
ATHEISM
HOPELESS HYPOTHESES OF
IS TRUE...
DAWKINS AND CO.
BRIAN JOHNSTON

Written by a nuclear scientist turned missionary, this book draws together some of Brian's previously published writings on apologetics to produce a concerted offensive against what the apostle Paul would surely describe as the 'indefensible' arguments of the so-called 'New Atheists'.

The short chapters in Brian's usual conversational style serve as an ideal entry-level primer for anyone wanting to get to grips with one of the most important of today's debates - or to use as an effective witnessing tool.

Also by Brian Johnston

Healthy Churches - God's Bible Blueprint For Growth
Hope for Humanity: God's Fix for a Broken World
First Corinthians: Nothing But Christ Crucified
Bible Answers to Listeners' Questions
Living in God's House: His Design in Action
Christianity 101: Seven Bible Basics
Nights of Old: Bible Stories of God at Work
Daniel Decoded: Deciphering Bible Prophecy
A Test of Commitment: 15 Challenges to Stimulate Your Devotion to Christ
John's Epistles - Certainty in the Face of Change
If Atheism Is True...
Brian Johnston Box Set 1
8 Amazing Privileges of God's People: A Bible Study of Romans 9:4-5
Learning from Bible Grandparents
Increasing Your Christian Footprint

About the Author

Born and educated in Scotland, Brian worked as a government scientist until God called him into full-time Christian ministry on behalf of the Churches of God (www.churchesofgod.info). His voice has been heard on Search For Truth radio broadcasts for over 30 years during which time he has been an itinerant Bible teacher throughout the UK and Canada. His evangelical and missionary work outside the UK is primarily in Belgium and The Philippines. He is married to Rosemary, with a son and daughter.